START-A-CRAFT

Decorative Tiling

Get started in a new craft with easy-to-follow

projects for beginners

PAUL HENRY

CHARTWELL
BOOKS, INC.

A QUINTET BOOK

Published by Chartwell Books
A Division of Book Sales, Inc.
P.O. Box 7100
Edison, New Jersey 08818-7100

This edition produced for sale
in the U.S.A., its territories
and dependencies only.

ISBN 0-7858-0321-1

This book was designed and produced by
Quintet Publishing Limited
6 Blundell Street
London N7 9BH

Creative Director: Richard Dewing
Designer: James Lawrence
Project Editor: Claire Tennant-Scull
Editor: Lydia Darbyshire
Photographer: Nick Bailey

Typeset in Great Britain by
Central Southern Typesetters,Eastbourne
Manufactured in Singapore by Eray Scan Pte. Ltd.
Printed in China by Leefung-Asco Printers Ltd.

CONTENTS

INTRODUCTION

Tiles are attractive to look at, permanent, easy to maintain, and extraordinarily versatile. They are also one of the oldest forms of decorative surface, familiar to us all, whether from illustrations of ancient Babylonian gateways or Victorian interiors. Although they are usually seen on large, flat surfaces, especially on walls in kitchens and bathrooms, there is no reason why they should not be used in other areas of the home, or to produce decorative objects in their own right. They have been widely used for many years in warm countries, especially those around the Mediterranean, but even in cooler countries, now that central heating is becoming so widespread, there is no reason that tiles cannot be used throughout the home in all kinds of ways. This book has been designed to show how tiles can be used relatively easily to produce a variety of ornamental objects. Once you have mastered the techniques involved, you will be able to use the ideas on the pages that follow to inspire you to try tiles in other, more adventurous and imaginative ways.

MATERIALS AND EQUIPMENT

Ceramic tiles are widely available from countless suppliers in an enormous range of styles and sizes. As a matter of fact, choosing tiles can be a daunting experience. Once you have made your selection, however, the skills needed are straightforward and easy to learn, and you are likely already to have most of the tools you will need in your standard household tool kit.

If there is one near your home, it is probably worth visiting a specialized tile shop. Not only will you be able to look at a vast range of tiles, but you will also be able to ask for advice about using them in the best possible ways.

BELOW: **It is worth investing in a tile cutter for accuracy and convenience.**

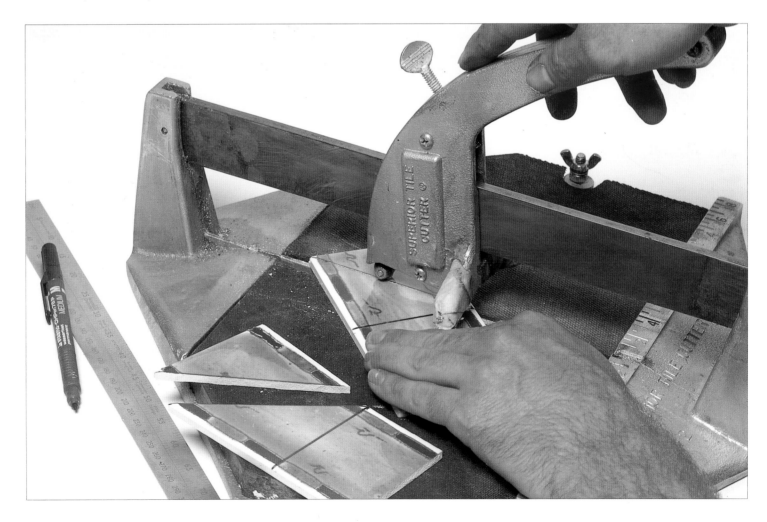

TILES

At their most basic, ceramic tiles are flat slabs of fired clay, usually covered with a glaze to protect the surface, or with a decoration of some kind. They are hard and brittle, but extremely durable. They range in size from mosaic pieces about ¾-inch square to floor tiles that are 12-inches square; floor tiles are often, but not always, larger than wall tiles. Rectangular tiles are becoming increasingly popular, although they have always been successfully used in public areas such as subway stations. Interlocking shapes are also sometimes used for floors. Tiles may be plain colored, screen printed, handpainted, or decorated by a combination of techniques. Raised images are sometimes incorporated, especially to give a period or traditional appearance to an area.

WALL TILES

There are practically no limits to the size, colors, and designs of wall tiles, but they are most often about either 4- or 6-inches square, with the larger squares being most widely used. You will, therefore, find the greatest range of designs and colors in this size.

TIP
• When drilling a hole in a tile, place masking tape over the tile to stop the drill from slipping.

MOSAIC TILES

Small tiles are generally known as mosaics, and they were used in the past for large, decorative panels in churches and other public buildings. Although they may be made of ceramic, they are often made of glass, and they are usually sold in sheets of a single color. Most are square, although interlocking shapes are also available. Ceramic mosaics are hard-wearing, and can be used for floors in entrance halls, where they can be arranged to create images or even names. Glass mosaics are more often used on walls or in swimming pools, and they are not available in such a wide range of colors as the ceramic equivalents.

BORDER TILES

There are few better ways of enlivening a room than by introducing some of these brightly colored strips, which are enjoying something of a revival. They are usually available in lengths of 6 or 8 inches, in almost every possible width, and they can be used to edge any other size of tile.

EMBOSSED OR RAISED TILES

Although these tend to be slightly more expensive than plain tiles, they are widely available and they are worth using to give an extra special finish.

TIP

• Cut tiles have surprisingly sharp edges, so take care that you do not nick your fingers as you handle them. Clear away any broken pieces immediately to avoid accidents.

TOOLS

Only a few tools are needed for tiling, and they are all readily available from local hardware shops, do-it-yourself stores, or tile shops.

You will need:

◊ Tile cutter (see below)
◊ Steel ruler, both to measure and to guide the hand-held cutter
◊ Waterproof pen to write on glazed surface of tiles

◊ Tile nippers (sharp, pincer-type tools) to nibble away small pieces from a tile
◊ Carborundum stone to smooth away sharp edges and to help ease the fit; always use a carborundum stone with water for best results

You must have a good tile cutter, of which two kinds are generally sold: plier-cutters and bench-cutters. A plier-cutter has a diamond or tungsten carbide tip or wheel, which is used to scribe lines. The other end of the tool, which has plier jaws, is used to snap the tile carefully along the scribed line. Unfortunately, these tools do not have very long lives; make sure you have some spare tips before you embark on any large projects. A bench-cutter is useful if you are cutting a large number of right angles or a batch of similar shapes. The tool is used to scribe the tile, which then, with downward pressure, can be snapped quite easily. This kind of cutter is useful if you are using heavy tiles, or if you cannot exert much pressure with your hands.

TILE CEMENT

Premixed cement is probably the easiest kind to use, and it is available in non-slip and waterproof versions. You will usually need about 2 pints of adhesive for each square yard of tiles. Spreading combs are often supplied with the cement, but make sure that you use one that feels comfortable in your hand and that is not too large for the area to be tiled.

GROUT

It is probably best to buy grout in powder form and to mix it with water as you need it. Recently an all-in-one adhesive and grout has become available, which does double duty and which you may prefer to use. Always read the manufacturer's instructions before you begin.

TILE SPACERS

Small plastic crosses are the most popular kind of tile spacer, which are used to make sure that all the tiles are evenly spaced; they are left between the tiles and grouted over. You can use matchsticks instead.

OTHER EQUIPMENT

The projects in this book also require the use of some other tools. Even if you do not already have them in your existing tool kit, you will find them in most building supply and general hardware shops.

◊ Small hammer
◊ Selection of brads and finishing nails
◊ Hand or power drill, with a selection of bits suitable for wood
◊ PVA-based wood glue; choose a quick-drying kind if available
◊ Sandpaper; you will need various grades
◊ Paint and paintbrushes; both oil- and water-based paints are used in different projects
◊ Steel ruler and pencil for measuring and marking wooden frames and battens
◊ Carpenter's level; essential for fixing the batten for the first row of tiles but useful in other projects, too
◊ Fine tenon saw and miter box to give frames true right-angled corners
◊ Small frame clamps (cramps)

BASIC WALL TILING

It is not the purpose of this book to explain all about wall tiling – there are plenty of good do-it-yourself guides available – but here are the key points.

You will need
◊ Carpenter's level
◊ Pencil
◊ Batten
◊ Ruler or measuring tape
◊ Hammer and fine nails
◊ Tiles
◊ Tile cement and comb
◊ Spacers
◊ Grout

TIP

- Always make sure that the surface to be tiled is sound, because tiles are considerably heavier than most other forms of wall covering. Wash the surface with warm water and detergent before you begin to tile.

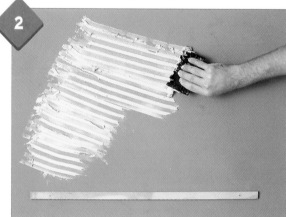

1 Use a level to establish a horizontal line, and fix a batten on the wall at the level of the first full row of tiles. This might not be the base of the wall but, because it is better to finish with a complete, uncut row of tiles, do some preparatory measuring.

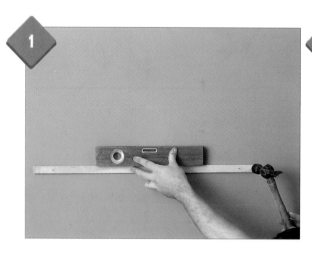

2 Use a notched comb to spread tile cement over the wall. Do not cover more than about 5 square feet at a time.

3 Press each tile firmly to the cement with a slight twisting action to make sure that there is full contact between the tile, the cement ,and the wall.

4 Place spacers at each corner to make sure that the grout lines are even, pressing the spacers firmly against the wall since they will be left in place and grouted over.

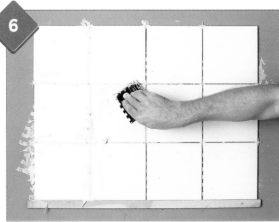

5 Continue to fix tiles in place, cleaning off any cement that is left on the front of the tiles before it dries and becomes hard to remove.

6 Leave the cement to dry, preferably overnight, then spread grout into the gaps between the tiles.

7 Smooth the joins with a finger, and add more grout if necessary.

TIP

• If you have to cut tiles, try to make sure that the cut pieces are as large as possible, and fit them into the least noticeable positions.

8 When the grout is set, polish the tiles with a clean, dry cloth.

STENCILED FLOWERS

If you feel like a change of decor but don't have sufficient funds to allow you to retile a whole wall with patterned tiles, a semi-permanent solution is to use enamel paints to decorate some plain tiles, or even to give existing tiles a new lease of life.

You will need
◊ Plain tiles
◊ Stencils (cut out from the templates on page 48)
◊ Masking tape
◊ White tiles for mixing colors
◊ Cold ceramic paints – red, yellow, and green
◊ Stencil brushes
◊ Utility knife
◊ Tile cement and comb
◊ Border tiles
◊ Grout

1 Use masking tape to hold the stencil in position on a tile.

2 Mix a range of greens from the yellow and green on a spare white tile. The different shades will enhance the overall appearance of the motifs.

3 Carefully apply the green paint with an upright stencil brush. Use only a little paint at a time. If you overload the brush, the paint will smudge around the edges.

TIP

• A range of cold enamel paints has been specially produced for use on ceramics, but although the paints will last for several years if treated with care and cleaned gently, they are not permanent. You can clean them off completely with a solvent and paint on new decorations if you wish. They are not suitable for use on tiles in places where they are likely to become wet – in showers, for example – although you can use them in other areas of the bathroom that do not become wet.

4 Mix red and green to make brown for the stem, and apply as before.

5 Leave the paint to dry for a few moments before lifting the stencil.

TIP

- Do not mix too much of any one color at a time because the paint dries quickly.

6 Use the other designs to decorate as many tiles as you need. You can remove any smudges of paint with a utility knife before the paint is set, then leave overnight for the paint to dry completely.

7 Use a notched comb to spread tile cement over the area to be tiled.

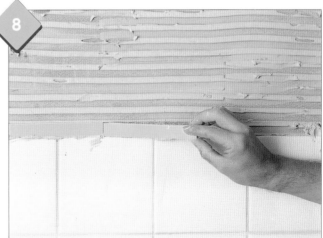

8 Fix the border tiles to the wall. Stagger the joins for best results.

9 Add the decorated tiles above the row of border tiles, making sure that they are pressed firmly against the wall. Add another row of border tiles before fixing any additional plain tiles that are required. Leave the tile cement to set overnight.

10 Spread grout into the spaces between the tiles, trying to avoid getting grout on the decorated areas. Make sure that the joins are completely filled, adding more grout if necessary.

11 Leave the grout to dry, then polish with a clean, dry cloth.

DECORATING A TILED WALL

• You can work directly onto an already tiled wall. Make sure that the surface is completely clean, and just before you begin stenciling, wipe it over with methylated spirit to remove any traces of grease. Take great care when you apply the colors not to overload your brushes, and leave each color to dry before you apply a new shade in order to avoid smudging.

TRADITIONAL HALL PANEL

Many Victorian and turn-of-the-century houses in Britain have decorative tiled panels on each side of the front door. There is no reason these panels should be confined to porches, however; they would be ideal in a conservatory or a bathroom, or even set into a tiled wall as a special feature.

You will need

◊ 2 sets of decorative picture tiles
   (10 6 x 6-inch tiles)
◊ Additional tiles and border strips to
   complement the picture tiles
◊ Tile cutter
◊ Carpenter's level
◊ Batten, hammer, and nails
◊ Tile cement and comb
◊ Sponges
◊ Grout

1 Measure the area to be tiled, and lay out the various tiles on a large, flat area so that you can double-check the measurements. Cut tiles to size if necessary.

2 Use a level to establish a horizontal line, and fix a batten to the wall.

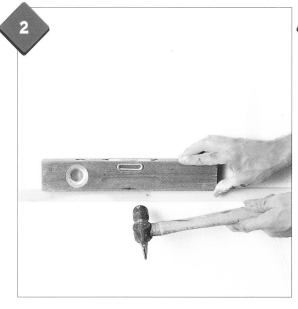

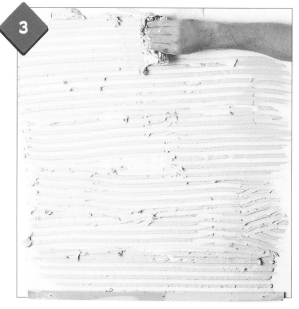

3 Spread tile cement over the area to be tiled with a notched comb.

4

TIP

• If the panel is going to be attached outdoors, make sure that you use a waterproof tile cement that is recommended for outside use.

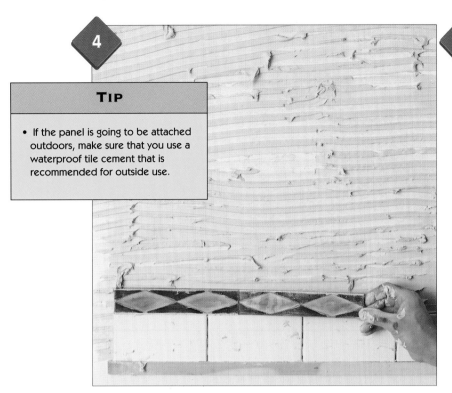

5

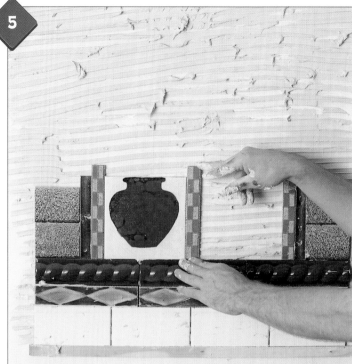

4 Beginning with the bottom tiles in your design, press each tile firmly to the cement with a slight twisting action.

5 Work upward in horizontal rows to ensure that the joins are even. It is more difficult to make fine adjustments if you apply the tiles in vertical rows.

6

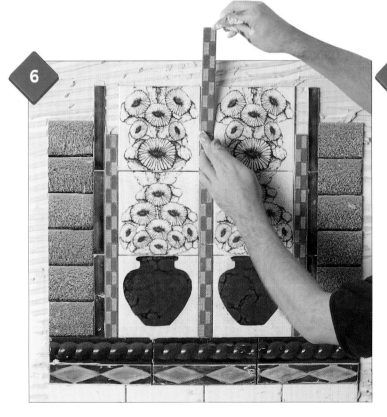

7

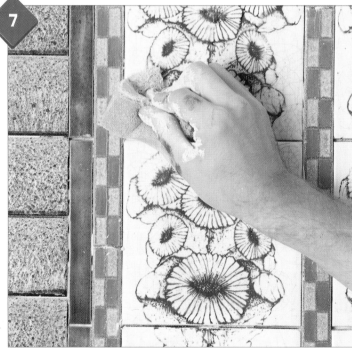

6 As you apply each picture tile, check that it is the right way up. It is all too easy to position tiles the wrong way around and not to notice until it is too late!

7 Continue to position the tiles, using a sponge to remove any cement from the front of the tiles before it sets.

8 When the tile cement is dry, carefully remove the batten and make good the surface. Spread grout over the entire pattern, taking care that all the joins are filled. Wipe off the surplus with a damp sponge, checking that all the joins are smooth.

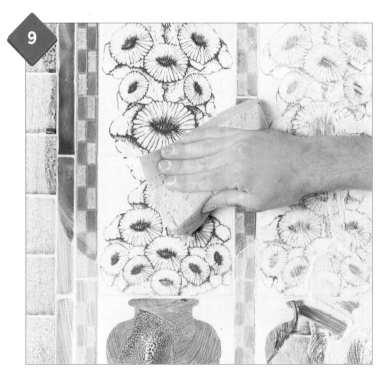

9 Leave the grout to dry, then polish the surface with a clean, dry cloth to remove any remaining traces.

CHESSBOARD

This board is the perfect foil for a special set of chessmen, although it can, of course, also be used for checkers. Alternatively, it could even be used as a stand for plants. The project is ideal for beginners because none of the tiles needs to be cut, and only basic woodworking skills are required.

You will need

◊ 1 square of ¼-inch plywood, 16 x 16 inches
◊ Drill with fine bit
◊ 4 wooden knobs for feet
◊ Screws
◊ Wooden edging strip, 6 feet long
◊ PVA wood adhesive
◊ Brad nails
◊ Tile cement and comb
◊ 64 mosaic tiles (32 of each color), each tile 2 x 2 inches
◊ Grout
◊ Wood stain

TIP

• If you cannot find mosaic tiles, cut small squares from larger tiles. Do this slowly and carefully because it is vital that each cut tile is absolutely square.

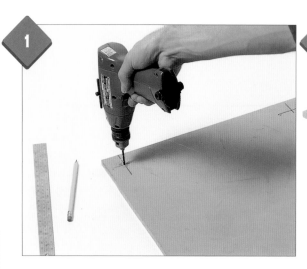

1 Mark the positions for the feet, slightly inset from the corners of the plywood square, and drill locating holes with a fine bit.

2 Attach the feet with screws through the locating holes.

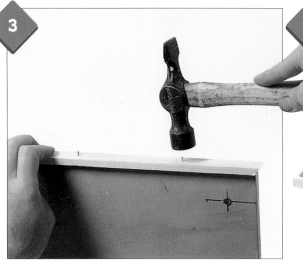

3 Measure and cut lengths of edging strip, and attach them to the sides of the plywood with wood adhesive and brads. The bottom edge of each strip should be flush with the base of the board.

4 Use a notched comb to spread tile cement over the board, making sure that you apply the cement right up to the edges.

5 Beginning with a light colored tile in the bottom right-hand corner, lay the tiles alternately. When you have filled the board, press each tile firmly in place.

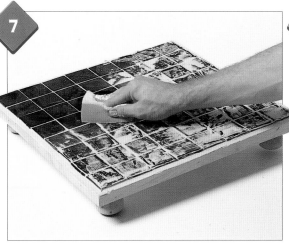

6 Leave the tile cement to set, then spread grout over the surface.

7 Wipe off any surplus grout with a damp sponge, making sure that the joins are smooth and well filled, and that there is no grout on the wood.

8 Leave the grout to dry before painting the edging strip and feet with wood stain to protect them.

TABLE STAND

Tiles are often used because they are durable, but they are also heat-resistant, which makes them ideal for use as stands for hot pans and teapots. Rather than using a single old tile, consider making a frame for an attractive tile so that you can place it on the dining table.

You will need

◊ 1⅛ x 1½-inch wooden molding, 5 feet long
◊ Saw
◊ PVA wood adhesive
◊ Clamps
◊ 1 decorative tile, 8 x 8 inches
◊ ¼ x ⅞-inch wooden strip, 32 inches long
◊ Hammer and nails
◊ Base color paint and picture frame rubbing gold
◊ Paintbrush
◊ Silicone sealant

1 Cut the molding into four pieces with mitered corners so that each has an internal length of slightly more than 8 inches to make fitting the tile easier.

2 Glue a corner and hold the frame pieces together with clamps, using small scraps of wood to prevent the clamps from marking the frame.

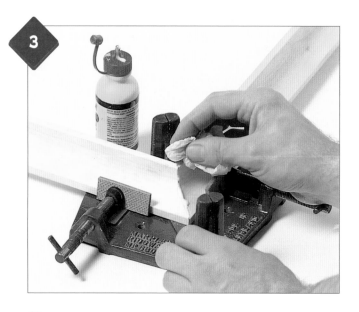

3 Use a damp cloth to wipe off any surplus adhesive, and leave to dry.

4 Repeat steps 2 and 3 on the other three corners. This may take some time.

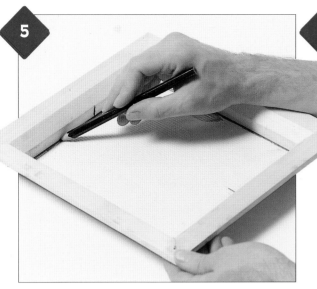

5 Place the tile on a flat surface, and turn the frame upside down over the tile. Mark on the frame the level of the tile as a guide for positioning the support.

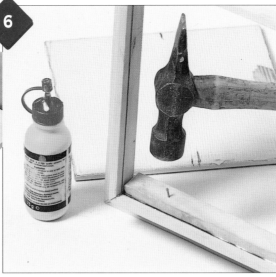

6 Cut the wooden strip into four lengths to fit inside the frame. Glue and nail the lengths to the frame so that the upper edges are flush with the marked line.

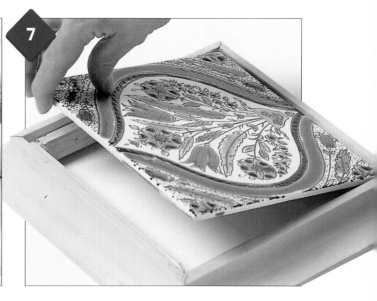

7 Check that the tile rests firmly on the supports.

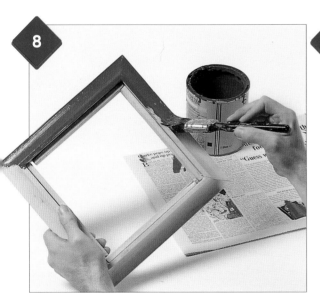

8 Remove the tile and paint the frame with the base color of your choice. Allow to dry.

9 Use your fingers to apply an even coat of frame rubbing gold to the external sides of the frame.

10 Leave the rubbing gold to dry, then carefully rub it back with a dry sponge to reveal traces of the base coat.

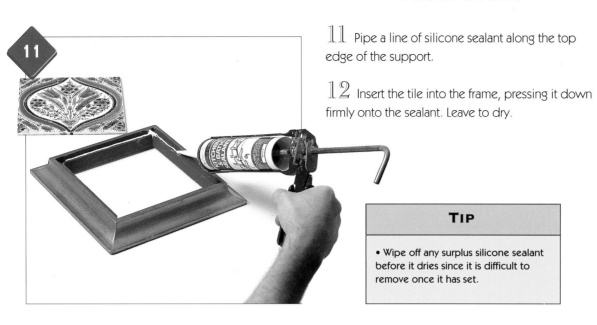

11 Pipe a line of silicone sealant along the top edge of the support.

12 Insert the tile into the frame, pressing it down firmly onto the sealant. Leave to dry.

TIP

• Wipe off any surplus silicone sealant before it dries since it is difficult to remove once it has set.

SMALL TRAY

Small trays are always useful, whether it is for serving drinks, for a few mugs of coffee and a plate of cookies, or for arranging sandwiches or light snacks. You can make the tray as large as you wish, but remember that the tiles themselves are relatively heavy, and this factor will limit the final size.

You will need
◊ 3 decorative tiles, each 6 x 6 inches
◊ Approximately 5 feet of wooden molding
◊ Saw
◊ PVA wood adhesive
◊ Clamps
◊ 1 piece of 4mm ⅛ inch plywood, approximately 18⅓ x 6⅓ inches
◊ Water-based paints in 2 colors
◊ Craquelle varnish
◊ Silicone sealant
◊ Hammer and brad nails

1 Measure the molding against a tile, and mark the positions of the miters.

2 Cut the wood so that you have two pieces with inside edges of 6 inches, and two pieces with inside edges of 18 inches. These sizes are only approximate: you must base the cutting marks on the dimensions of the tiles you are actually using.

3 Glue together the cut edges of a long piece and a short piece with PVA wood adhesive.

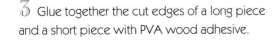

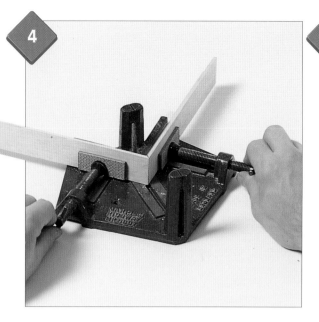

4 Clamp the two pieces together, using scraps of wood to stop the clamps marking the molding. Wipe off any surplus adhesive before it sets, then leave to dry.

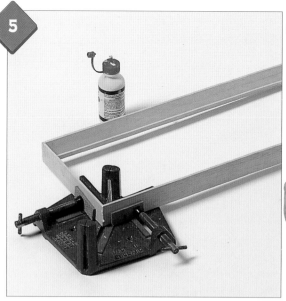

5 Repeat steps 3 and 4 at the other three corners, leaving the adhesive to dry each time. Trim the plywood base so that it fits exactly into the base of the frame.

6 Paint the entire frame and one side of the base in base color; allow to dry. Apply a coat of craquelle varnish and leave to dry, preferably overnight.

7 Apply a coat of the second color, painting it on in quick, confident strokes so that you do not disturb the craquelle. Leave to dry.

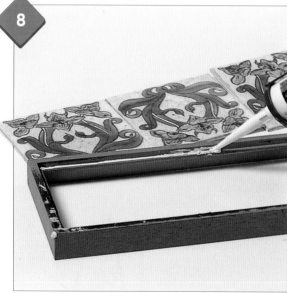

8 Turn the frame upside down, and pipe a line of silicone sealant along the edge of the rebate.

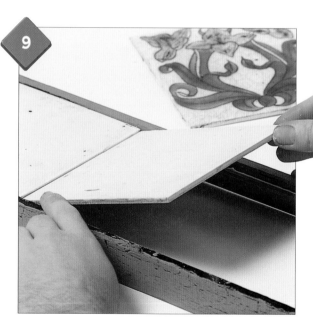

9 Carefully insert the tiles, face down and in the correct order, into the frame, pressing them down firmly onto the sealant. Remove any surplus sealant from the surface of the tiles, then leave to dry.

TIP

• When you paint a frame, make sure that you also paint the inside rebate in case it shows around the outside edges of the tiles.

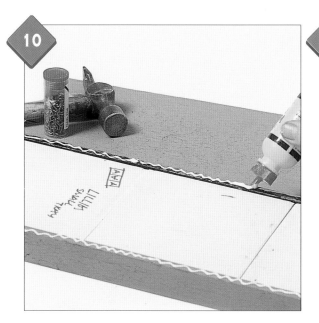

10 Apply a wavy line of wood adhesive to the edge of the frame.

11 Position the baseboard over the frame, wiping away any surplus adhesive before it dries.

12 Use small steel brads to fix the edge of the baseboard to the frame.

FRAMED PANEL

◆

Handpainted tiles can be used with plain tiles when you are covering a wall, but you may be unwilling to fix such pretty tiles in place permanently. One solution is to frame them and use them as a picture so that you can move them around, either if you move house or simply to change the decor of a room. The materials quoted here are for a 12-tile panel, but they can be simply adjusted to accommodate the tiles of your choice. Because the frame itself is so light, no special fixing method is necessary, which is an additional advantage.

You will need
◊ 1 x 1 inch wooden strip, 11 feet long
◊ Saw and miter box
◊ PVA wood adhesive
◊ Clamps
◊ 12 decorative tiles, each 6 x 6 inches
◊ Hammer, nails, and brads
◊ 2 pieces of ¼-inch plywood, each 18 x 4 inches
◊ Silicone sealant
◊ Grout and spreader
◊ Hockey stick molding, 7½ feet long
◊ Liquid wood wax
◊ 2 screw eyes and wire or string for hanging

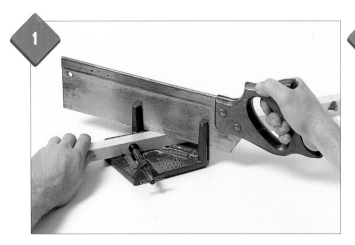

1 Using the miter box, cut two strips of wood, each 18 inches long on the longest edge, with both ends mitered in opposite directions. Then cut two strips of wood, each 2 feet long on the longest edge, with both ends mitered in opposite directions. Cut two strips of wood, each 22 inches long, with square ends.

2 Glue the mitered corner of one short piece to the mitered end of a long piece, clamping them in the miter frame until the adhesive is set. Repeat with the remaining mitered corners to make a frame, leaving the adhesive to dry completely each time. The frame should have the exact measurements of the outside dimensions of the tile panels.

3 Use one of the tiles to mark on the short sides of the frame the position of the center of the two vertical struts.

4 Position the two vertical pieces on the pencil marks before gluing and nailing into place.

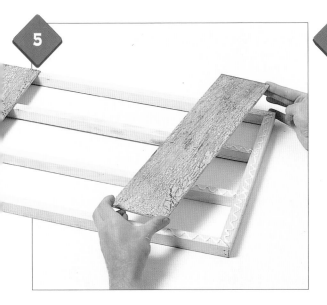

5 Apply a line of wood adhesive along the shorter ends of the two rectangles of plywood, and glue them to the ends of the frame.

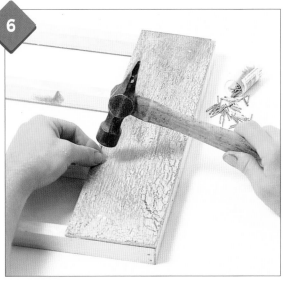

6 Nail the plywood to the underlying struts to give additional stability to the frame. Leave to dry overnight.

7 Apply the silicone sealant in wavy lines to the top side of the frame.

8 Begin to position the tiles on the sealant. When all the tiles are in place, adjust the spacing if necessary. Do not use tile spacers, which would leave too great a gap between each tile. Remove any surplus sealant from the surface of the tiles, and leave to dry for at least 4 hours.

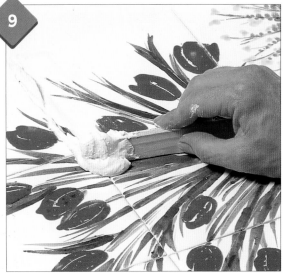

9 Apply grout to the joins with a spreader, and leave for about 10 minutes so that it dries slightly. Clean off the grout, using a finger to press the grout between the joins, and use a damp sponge to remove all traces of grout. This can take several attempts.

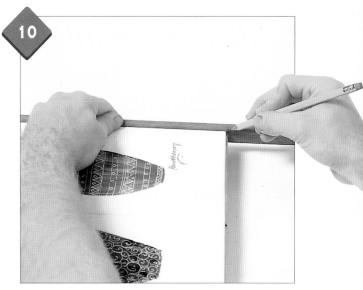

10 Measure the hockey stick molding against the outside edge of the frame to get an exact fit.

11 Cut the molding to length, mitering the corners and making sure that the mitered cuts are in opposite directions at each end of each piece.

12 Apply a line of adhesive to the edge of the frame, then use small brads to tack the molding to the frame.

13 Seal the molding with liquid wax, taking care not to get the wax on the face of the tiles. When it is dry, buff it with a dry cloth.

14 Turn over the panel and fix two screw eyes to the frame, about one-third of the way down from the top, before attaching the wire or string.

GAUDI-STYLE PLANTER

The Spanish architect Antoni Gaudi (1852–1926) is probably best remembered for his work in Barcelona, especially the garden he created at Guell Park, which was constructed from thousands of broken tiles. Even if we had the space, such a project is far too ambitious for most of us, but these planters can be made to pay homage to Gaudi's individual style and to act as a reminder of Spain. It is also an ideal way of using broken tiles. It doesn't matter if they are patterned, but they must have a distinct color.

You will need
◊ 1 12-inch terracotta flowerpot
◊ Metal ruler and felt-tipped pen
◊ Selection of broken tiles
◊ Sacking or burlap and heavy hammer
◊ Tile cement for exterior use and spreader
◊ Rubber gloves
◊ Tile nippers

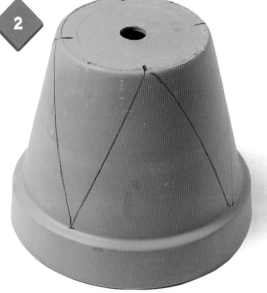

1 Turn the flowerpot upside down, and mark on the base four equidistant points. Midway between the four original points, mark four more points on the bottom of the rim.

2 Join the marks to create a series of triangles. Make sure that the triangles around the flowerpot are clearly drawn in.

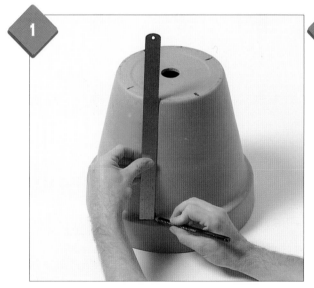

3 Wrap several tiles, all of the same color, in a piece of sacking, and hit them with a heavy hammer. You need fairly small pieces, none larger than about 2 inches in any direction.

4

4 Apply tile cement to one of the triangles. Make sure to wear rubber gloves since the cement may irritate your skin.

5

5 Begin to position the tiles, placing the straight edges along the sides of the triangles.

6

6 Continue to fill the triangle. You may need to cut small pieces to fit into the apex.

TIP

• Keep the same colors together when you break the tiles, otherwise you will spend a lot of time sorting them out.

TIP

• Do not be tempted to try to use large pieces of tile. The cement will not cushion them, and the surface of the finished planter will be jagged and difficult to handle without cutting your hands.

7

7 Complete two or three sections, using different colors in each, then use a spreader to cover the tile pieces with a layer of cement. This will fill in any gaps and act as a grout.

8

8 Use a wet sponge to remove the surplus cement, checking that all the gaps are completely filled.

9 Continue to work around the flowerpot. Pay particular attention to the points at what will be the base. The tile pieces must not protrude, or the flowerpot will not be stable when it is turned the right way up.

10 Check that all holes are filled, using extra cement as necessary, then use a damp sponge to remove all surplus cement. Take care to clean off any cement from the terracotta pot – it is difficult to remove when it has hardened. Leave for 24 hours for the cement to harden completely.

SUN AND MOON PANEL

Tiled rooms can sometimes appear very plain, especially if a limited budget has meant that you have used tiles of a single color to cover a large area. This project, which would be ideal for a kitchen or bathroom, uses just a few colored tiles to create an eye-catching feature. The quantities quoted are for one sun and one moon, but you could use several motifs in the same room.

You will need
◊ 8 white tiles, each 6 x 6 inches
◊ 3 yellow tiles, each 6 x 6 inches
◊ 1 orange tile, 6 x 6 inches
◊ Draftsman's compass and felt-tipped pen
◊ Tile cutter
◊ Tile nippers
◊ Carborundum stone
◊ Cold ceramic paint – brown
◊ Stencil brush
◊ Tile cement and comb
◊ Grout

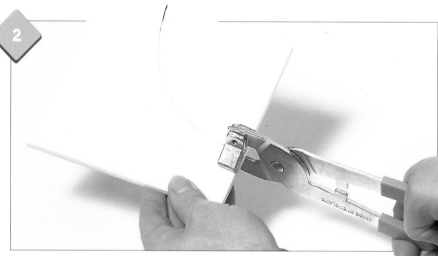

1 Lay four tiles in a square and, using the center point, draw a circle with a radius of 2 inches so that each tile has a quadrant of the circle marked on it. Scribe the line on each tile, pushing the cutter away from you so that you can see clearly the line you are following. Turn over a tile, and tap it roughly along the line you have scribed. This will help the tile snap along the line.

2 Gently squeeze the tile cutter to crack the tile. You can often hear the sound of the tile beginning to crack.

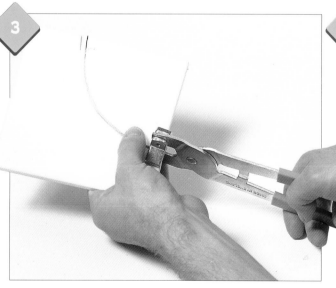

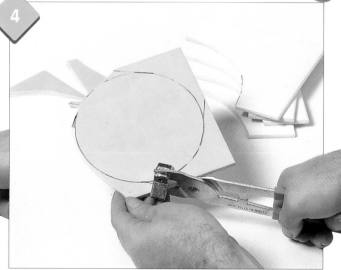

3 Snapping a tile along a curved line can be difficult, so be patient. Repeat on all four tiles, but with a radius of 2½ inches for the moon.

4 Using the template on page 47, trace a circle on a yellow tile. Scribe the outline of the circle, and cut away the pieces from the edge.

5 Use tile nippers to snap off the protruding edges to give a neat outline.

6 Smooth the edge with a carborundum stone. Make a second yellow circle in the same way for the moon.

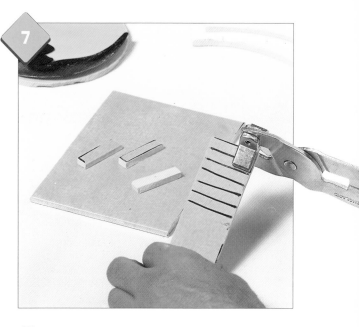

7 Cut strips 1 x ⅜ inch from orange and yellow tiles.

8 Stencil the moon's face onto one of the yellow circles using the special cold ceramic paint. Stencil the sun's face onto the other yellow circle. Leave the ceramic paint to harden overnight or the color will rub off at the next stage.

9 Lay out the pieces of the design on a flat surface to make sure that all the elements fit together. If necessary, trim the strips cut in step 8 so that they fit neatly around the sun's face.

10 Cement the white tiles with the cut-out sections to the wall, making sure that they form even circles.

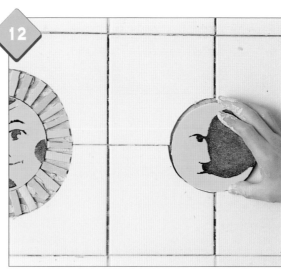

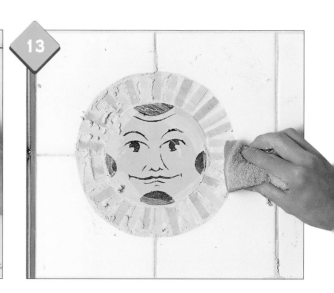

11 Position the sun in the center of the appropriate space. Carefully place alternate strips of orange and yellow around the sun's face, pressing each piece firmly against the wall.

12 Fit the moon's face into the other space.

13 Use grout to fill the spaces between the sun's rays and also all other exposed joins. It's best to apply the grout with a sponge because you will need a lot to fill all the spaces. Do not use your fingers; there are too many sharp edges, and you could easily cut yourself. The spaces between the rays will be slightly below the surface of the tiles when you have finished. Although the ceramic paint is fairly hardwearing, try to avoid getting any grout on the painted surfaces.

HOUSE NUMBER

Although it involves a lot of cutting, this is an easy project and a wonderful way of personalizing your home from the outside. Use whatever colors you like, although two contrasting tones will work best.

You will need

◊ 2 tiles, each 6 x 6 inches, in contrasting colors
◊ 1 plain tile, 6 x 6 inches
◊ Tile cutters
◊ Tile nippers
◊ Tracing paper and pencil
◊ Masking tape
◊ Felt-tipped pen
◊ Clear, self-adhesive plastic film
◊ Tile cement for exterior use and comb

1 On one of the colored tiles score a series of parallel lines, ½ inch apart. This is easiest to do with a bench-cutter, but a hand cutter and a heavy ruler will work well.

2 Turn the tile through 90 degrees and repeat step 1 to form a grid.

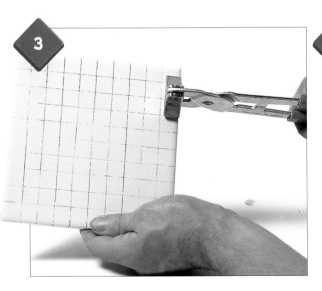

3 Use the plier-cutter end of the your tile cutter to break the tile into strips.

4 Break up each strip to make small squares.

5 Repeat the process with the other colored tile. Keep the colored squares in separate piles.

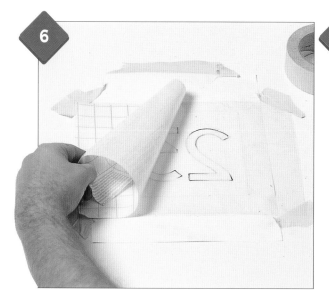

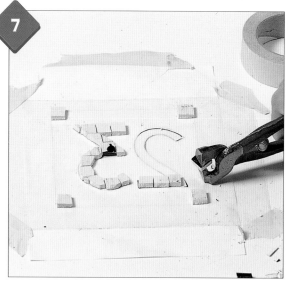

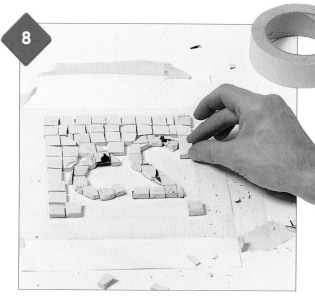

6 Trace your chosen number and lay the tracing paper face down on your work surface, holding it in place with masking tape. Go over the outlines, which will be in reverse, with a fine, felt-tipped pen. Cover the tracing paper with a sheet of adhesive film, sticky side upward, and hold it in place with masking tape.

7 Begin to fill in the shapes of the number with the dark tiles. You may have to cut the edges to make them fit neatly. Place the tiles face down.

8 Use the lighter tiles to fill in the background, arranging them so that they run more or less in horizontal rows. Cut pieces to size to fit the awkward gaps.

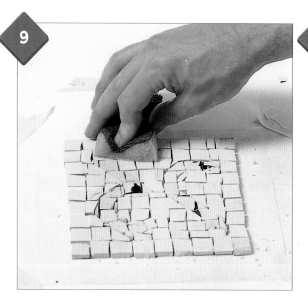

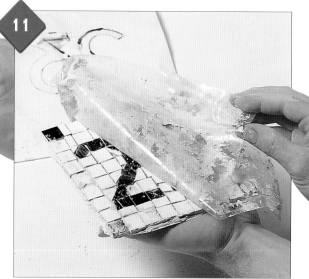

9 Lightly rub the back of the tile pieces with a damp sponge to remove all traces of dust. Take care that you do not allow the tiles to become too wet.

10 Carefully cover the back of the pieces with tile cement. This can be difficult as the individual pieces have a tendency to lift. Work slowly and patiently. Leave to dry overnight before attempting to move.

11 Turn over the tile and gently remove the plastic film.

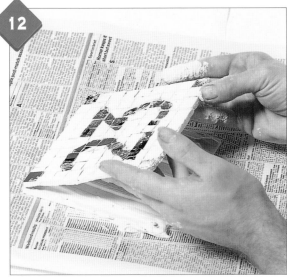

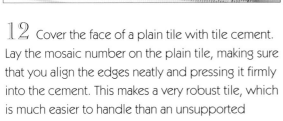

12 Cover the face of a plain tile with tile cement. Lay the mosaic number on the plain tile, making sure that you align the edges neatly and pressing it firmly into the cement. This makes a very robust tile, which is much easier to handle than an unsupported mosaic design.

13 Cover the face of the mosaic numbers with more cement. This will act as a grout, and will be more durable in an exposed position outdoors. If your number is going to be in a protected position such as in a porch, you could use grout instead.

14 Clean off all surplus cement with a sponge, paying particular attention to the surface of the number itself.

MIRROR FRAME

Few of us would admit to being vain, but there is no doubt that an extra mirror is always useful. This one, with its border of dolphins, would be perfect for a bathroom, but if you visit a specialized tile shop you are almost certain to find tiles that would suit almost any room.

You will need

◊ 2-inch x ¼ inch wooden strip, 6½ feet long
◊ Saw and miter box
◊ 1 piece of ¼-inch plywood, 18 x 18 inches
◊ 1 square mirror glass, 14 x 14 inches
◊ Ruler and pencil
◊ Bradawl
◊ 4 mirror corners and screws
◊ Screwdriver
◊ Silicone sealant
◊ PVA wood adhesive
◊ Hammer and brads
◊ 12 border tiles, each 6 x 3 inches
◊ Tile cutter
◊ Carborundum stone
◊ Grout
◊ 2 screw eyes

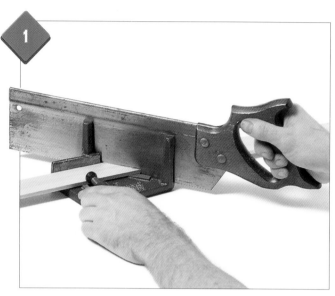

1 Cut four pieces of wooden strip with mitered corners so that they fit the edges of the plywood square.

2 Lay the strips along the edges of the base square, and position the mirror tile in the center. Mark the positions of the glass and strips on the plywood base.

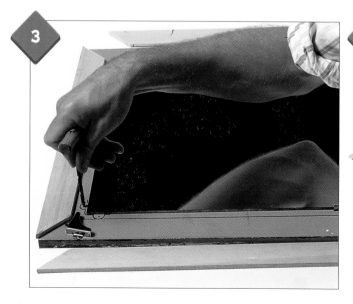

3 Use a bradawl to mark the positions for the screws for the mirror corners.

4 With the mirror in place, screw the mirror corners to the baseboard.

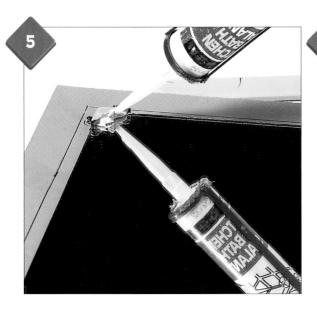

5 Fill the mirror corners with small amounts of silicone sealant to cushion the mirror. This is not always necessary, but it does protect the corners of the mirror.

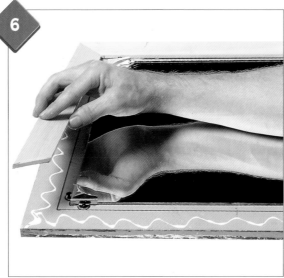

6 Use wood adhesive to attach the wooden strips around the mirror, making sure that the edges align with the outside edges of the base board.

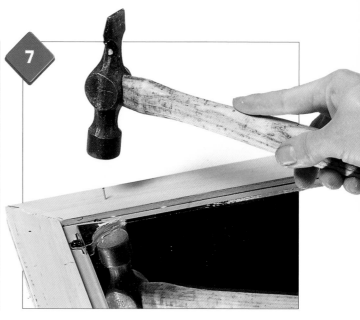

7 Tap in a few brads to make sure that the strips are firmly attached to the baseboard.

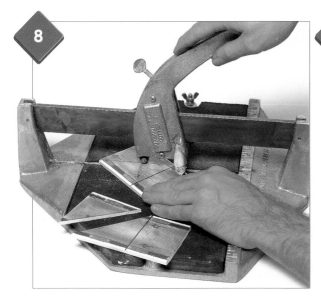

8 Use a tile cutter to cut four right-handed miter angles and four left-handed miter angles. Smooth the cut edges with a carborundum stone to make sure that they fit neatly together.

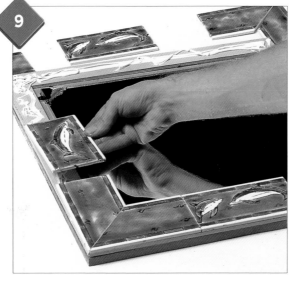

9 Cover the wooden edging strip with silicone sealant, and position the tiles. Adjust the tiles so that they are evenly spaced, then leave to dry overnight.

10 Apply grout to the tiles, making sure that it also covers the sides of the tiles that lie against the mirror. Clean away the grout with a finger as it begins to dry, then use a clean, damp sponge to remove the final traces. Fix two screw eyes to the back for hanging.

ART DECO FISH

Simple designs can be cut from tiles of contrasting colors to form interesting panels or borders. The process is time consuming, although it is much less expensive than buying specially decorated border tiles. Large and small geometric patterns can look extremely effective, but we have used a fish, which would be ideal in a bathroom.

You will need

◊ Tracing paper and pencil
◊ Cardboard
◊ Felt-tipped pen
◊ 2 white tiles, each 6 x 6 inches
◊ 2 black tiles, each 6 x 6 inches
◊ Tile cutter
◊ Tile nippers
◊ Carborundum stone
◊ Tile cement and comb
◊ Narrow border tiles
◊ Grout

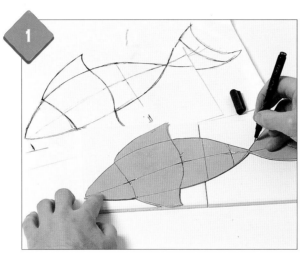

1 Transfer the fish pattern (see page 48) to a piece of cardboard, and use it to transfer the outline to the white tiles.

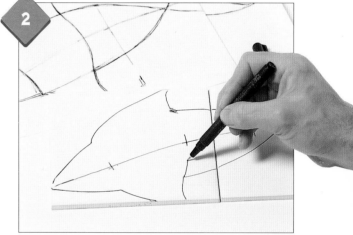

2 Join up the register marks by hand.

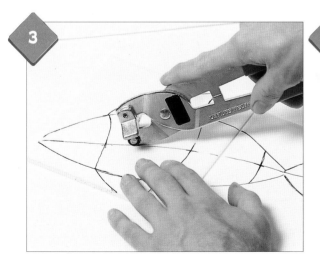

3 Carefully scribe along the marked lines, beginning with the longest cuts. Try to cut in one smooth action, and avoid jerky movements.

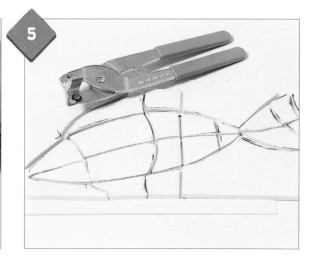

4 Tap the underside of the tiles and break along the scribed lines. If some cuts are not successful, you can always cut extra pieces from other tiles. Sometimes it seems as if tiles will not break just as you want them to.

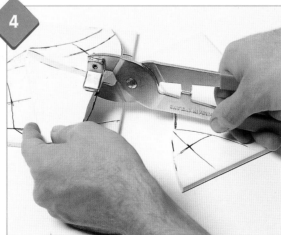

5 Lay out the pieces on top of the tracing to avoid confusion later on.

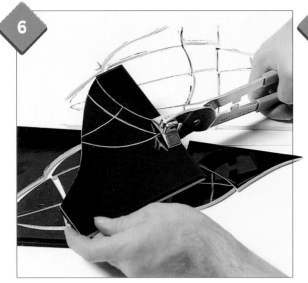

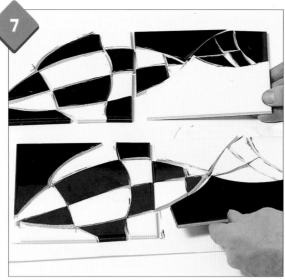

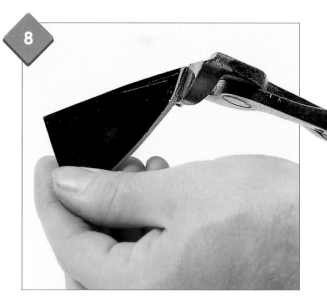

6 Repeat steps 1–5 inclusive with the black tiles.

7 Rearrange the black and white pieces to create a checkered design.

8 Use your tile nippers to remove any protruding pieces of tile.

TIP

• When you use border strips above plain tiles, try to stagger the vertical lines of the joins.

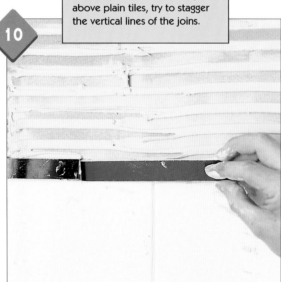

9 Smooth the rough edges with a carborundum stone, and make sure that the pieces fit neatly together. Remember to use water with the carborundum stone in order to prevent the edges from chipping.

10 Apply tile cement to a small area of the wall with a toothed scraper or comb, then start to position the tiles, beginning with the bottom row of border tiles.

11 Working from the left-hand side, position the mosaic pieces.

TIP

• When you are applying grout between cutout pieces of tile, use a sponge. It is very easy to cut your fingers on the sharp edges.

12 Continue to fix tile pieces, building up the motifs from left to right.

13 Finish off with another row of border tiles. Make sure that all the surfaces are flat, and that all the pieces are firmly pressed to the cement. Check that the spaces between the tile pieces are even, then clean any surplus cement from the surfaces of the tiles. Leave overnight for the cement to dry.

14 Use a sponge to apply the grout. Remove surplus grout from the surface of the tiles before it dries, making sure that all the joins are completely and neatly filled. When the grout is dry, clean the surface with a slightly damp sponge.

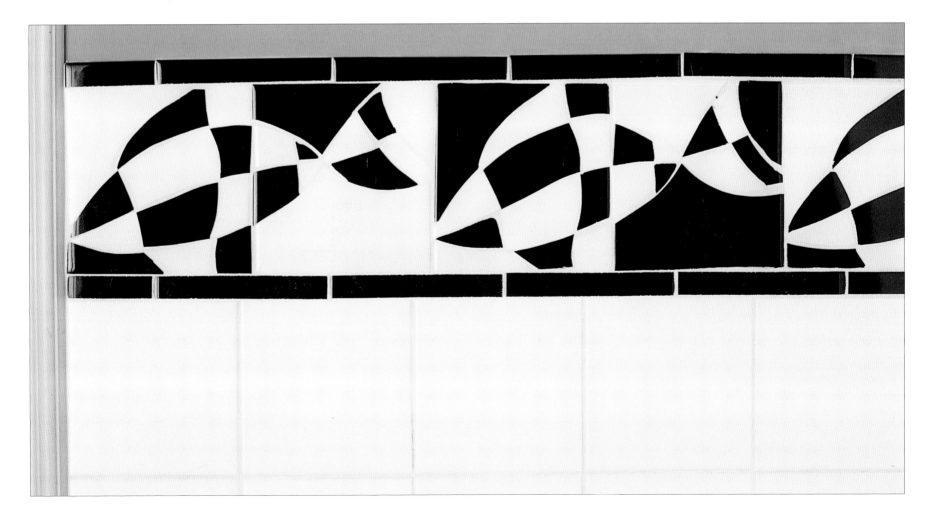

WINDOW BOX

A window box is a wonderful way of brightening up a dull windowsill, and this planter could be used indoors or out. We have used tiles with a fairly traditional floral pattern, but it would look equally stunning with geometric or abstract patterns. Although it is time-consuming, this project is well worth the effort.

You will need

◊ Saw and miter box
◊ 1 x 1 inch wooden strip, 15 feet long
◊ PVA wood adhesive
◊ Hammer and nails
◊ Clamps
◊ 1 piece of ¼-inch plywood,
   5½ feet x 10 inches
◊ Hockey stick molding, 3 feet long
◊ 2- x ⅜-inch wooden strip, 15 feet long
◊ Drill
◊ 8 small wooden knobs
◊ ¾- x ¼-inch wooden strip, 6 feet long
◊ Sandpaper
◊ Oil-based paint for exterior use
◊ Silicone sealant
◊ Grout

1 Use the saw and miter box to cut the length of square wooden strip into four pieces, two with an inside length of just over 24 inches, and two with an inside length of just over 6 inches.

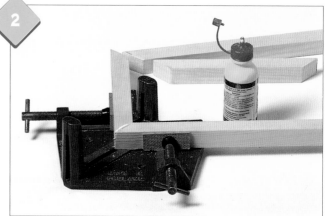

2 Check that the angles at each end of each piece run in opposite directions, then glue one short piece to one long piece with wood adhesive.

3 Clamp them together until the adhesive is dry, then use finishing nails diagonally across the corners for extra strength. Repeat steps 2 and 3 until the frame is complete.

4 Cut a piece of plywood to the exact dimensions of the frame. Glue and nail it to the frame, then leave to dry. Make a second frame with a plywood cover in exactly the same way. These are the two long sides of the window box.

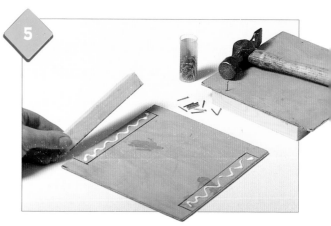

5 From the remaining plywood cut two squares, each 8 x 8 inches; from the 1- x 1-inch wooden strip cut four lengths, each 6 inches long. Glue and nail a strip along two opposite sides of each plywood square, positioning the strips in the center of the edges. These pieces form the two short sides.

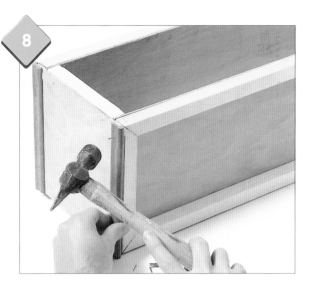

6 Glue and nail both short sides to a long side. Leave to dry.

7 Glue and nail the second long side to the short sides to create a box. Leave to dry.

8 Cut four pieces of hockey stick molding, each 8 inches long, and glue and tack a length of molding to each vertical corner edge.

9 Use the saw and miter box to cut the 2- x ⅜-inch wooden strip into four pieces, two with an inside length of just over 24 inches, and two with an inside length of just over 6 inches. Make sure that the angles at each end face in opposite directions. Making sure that the inside edge is flush with the inside of the box, glue and tack the pieces along the top edge of the frame to create a decorative ledge. Repeat to make an edging around the foot of the box.

10 Drill through the corners of the top ledge to make seating holes for the knobs. Glue a knob in each corner. Repeat at the four bottom corners to make feet.

11 From the ¾- x ¼-inch strip cut two lengths, each 26 inches long. Glue and tack the strips to the inside bottom ledge to provide supports for the pots.

TIP

• The materials quoted here are for a window box with four 6- x 6-inch tiles along each of the long sides. Larger or smaller versions can be easily made in the same way, however, by increasing or reducing the dimensions of the basic frame.

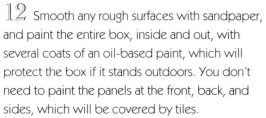

12 Smooth any rough surfaces with sandpaper, and paint the entire box, inside and out, with several coats of an oil-based paint, which will protect the box if it stands outdoors. You don't need to paint the panels at the front, back, and sides, which will be covered by tiles.

13 Apply silicone sealant to one long side, and firmly place four tiles in position. Leave to dry, then repeat on the other long side. Leave to dry.

14 Spread grout along the joins between and around the tiles, cleaning off any surplus grout before it dries hard. Leave to dry before using a clean, dry cloth to polish the tiles and remove the final traces of grout. Use an exterior grout if the window box is to be used outside.

TEMPLATES

The templates on the following pages are used to complete the Stenciled Flowers, Sun and Moon, and Art Deco Fish projects.

If you are using a different sized tile from those listed in this book, or if you would prefer to create your own designs from patterns and motifs that you have seen in a magazine, you may need to adjust the size. The easiest way of enlarging or decreasing the size of an outline is by photocopying, and many libraries, office supply shops, and stationery stores have photocopiers that can enlarge or reduce in a range of percentages.

If you do not have access to a photocopier, use the grid method. Use a sharp pencil and ruler to draw a series of evenly spaced, parallel lines horizontally and vertically across the image you wish to copy. It is usually easier if at least some of the grid lines touch the edges of the original shape. On a clean sheet of paper draw a second grid, but this time with the lines spaced at a proportionately greater distance. For example, if you wanted to double the size of the image, the lines on your first grid might be 1 inch apart on the original and 2 inches apart in your second grid. It is relatively simple to transfer the shapes in one square of the original grid to the corresponding square in the second grid. If the outline you want to copy is complicated, a smaller grid might be easier to use – ½-inch squares in the original and 1-inch squares in the larger version.

CUTTING STENCILS

When you are happy with the size of your image, go over the outlines with a fine felt-tipped pen. Then use either tracing paper or carbon paper to transfer the outline to stencil card.

Working on a special cutting mat or on a spare piece of thick cardboard, use a utility knife or scalpel to cut through the lines. Work slowly and carefully so that the cut lines are neat and accurate.

Carefully made stencils can be used time and again, especially if you take care to wipe away any paint that is left on them, using water or a solvent as appropriate, and then allow them to dry flat, away from direct heat.

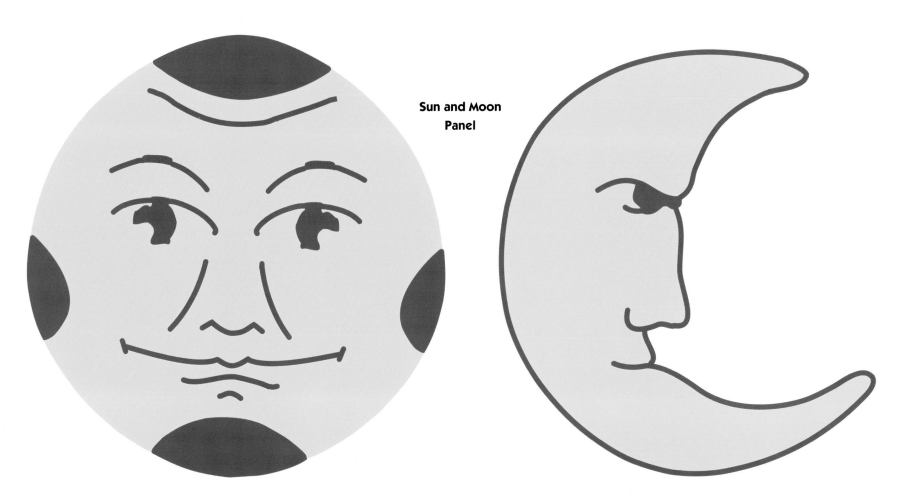

**Sun and Moon
Panel**

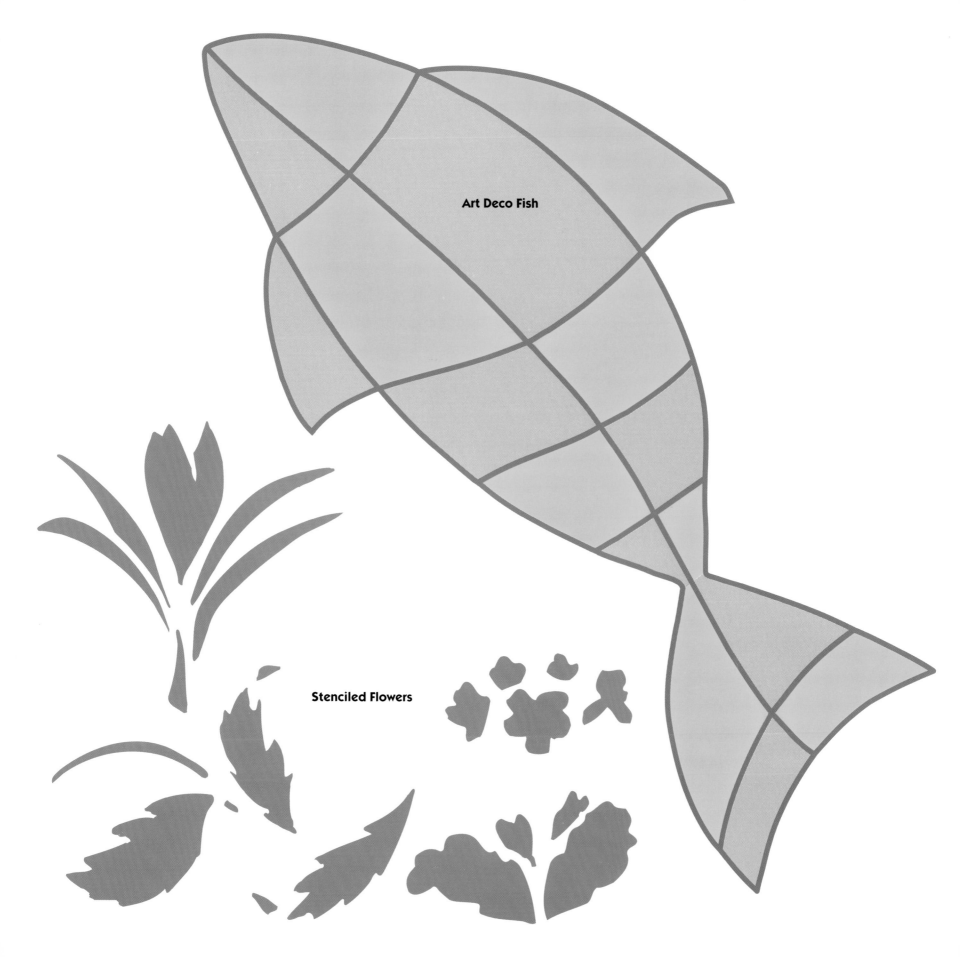

Art Deco Fish

Stenciled Flowers